*Heroes for Young Readers Activity Guides and audio CDs
are also available. See the back of this book for more information.*

HEROES FOR YOUNG READERS

DAVID LIVINGSTONE

Courageous Explorer

Written by Renee Taft Meloche
Illustrated by Bryan Pollard

David Livingstone: Courageous Explorer Text © 2004, 2018 by Renee Taft Meloche Illustrations © 2004 by Bryan Pollard
Published by YWAM Publishing, P.O. Box 55787, Seattle, WA 98155 ISBN 978-1-57658-238-1 Printed in China.

A twelve-year-old named David was
        excited as he hiked,
for when he reached the hilltop he
        could do just what he liked.

His precious book was hidden well,
        a science book on plants.
He felt it tied against his leg
        inside his trouser pants.

He looked down at his Scottish town
        once he had reached the top—
its crumbling houses made of brick
        and old and gloomy shops.

He saw the cotton mill where he
        worked long and hard each day.
His books helped him escape and dream
        of places far away.

He took his book out after he
    had first untied the string,
although his dad had warned him not
    to ever read such things.

The year was eighteen twenty-four
    and many Christians thought
that learning how things had been made
    should simply not be taught.

His grandpa still thought science books
    had knowledge that was good,
so secretly he lent them out
    to David when he could.

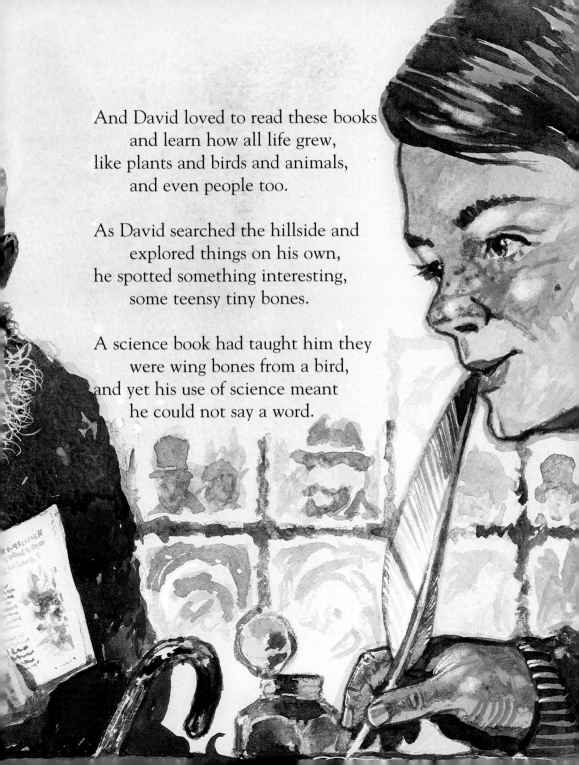

And David loved to read these books
and learn how all life grew,
like plants and birds and animals,
and even people too.

As David searched the hillside and
explored things on his own,
he spotted something interesting,
some teensy tiny bones.

A science book had taught him they
were wing bones from a bird,
and yet his use of science meant
he could not say a word.

But then a missionary spoke
    about work overseas:
"We need skilled doctors who've been taught
    both science and disease."

When David prayed he knew that this
    was something that felt right.
His father even changed his view
    of science that same night.

So David studied many years
    till he got his degree,
then took a ship to Africa
    across the mighty sea.

He stayed with Christians near the coast,
    yet soon he left that place
and headed inland where he did
    not know what he would face.

He took an ox and wagon and
    a native was his guide.
Not one white man had gone before.
    Not one had even tried.

For inland was a wilderness
    with dangers everywhere,
like animals and tribes who might
    attack a stranger there.

The wagon rumbled northward as
    snakes slithered in the dust.
Gazelles pranced by and elephants
    came trampling through the brush.

Then two weeks later David watched
    as Africans drew near.
They wore tanned leather tunics and
    they carried long, sharp spears.

They danced around the wagon and
    when it was time to go,
they steered his ox along a path.
    A valley lay below.

As David looked, he saw round huts
    with cone-shaped roofs of straw.
Small children stood in doorways as
    they shyly stared in awe.

Then David heard the loud and steady
    beating of some drums.
He turned around to see just where
    the sound was coming from.

A man who was surrounded by
    big warriors arrived.
It was the noble village chief,
    the leader of the tribe.

The chief wore lion's skin that had
    been turned into a cloak.
He looked a little scary as
    he slowly stood and spoke.

Though David did not understand,
    he felt a huge relief
when his guide told him afterwards,
    "We're welcomed by this chief."

A cow was killed that very night,
    which made a tasty roast.
The tribe then danced to please their guests,
    for they were gracious hosts.

The next day David grabbed his bag
    and asked the sick to come.
He took out different medicines
    to try to help each one.

He asked about their customs so
    that he could learn their ways,
and David treated many sick
    throughout the coming days.

As David headed north he met
    a chief with damaged eyes.
When David's ointment cured the chief,
    the chief looked so surprised.

His eyes were clear and he could see!
    His gratitude was great,
so he gave David in return
    a gift of meat to take.

It was a little farther on
        when David heard the sound
of someone sobbing underneath
        his wagon near the ground.

He got down on his knees and saw
        a young girl crouching low.
She wore long strands of colored beads
        and shook from head to toe.

She looked about eleven and
    as tears streamed down her face,
he slowly, gently got the girl
    to leave her hiding place.

She told him that her mom and dad
    and sister all had died.
Her uncle planned to sell her now
    and make her someone's bride.

Then David heard another noise—
    a warrior appeared.
The man had come to get the girl.
    Her eyes were full of fear.

So David stepped between them and
    became a human shield.
The tribesman talked to David's guide
    until they reached a deal.

The guide explained, "If she returns
    the beads she can go free."
Though they were used as money she
    unwound them willingly.

She gave them to the warrior.
    He left around the bend.
The grateful girl returned back home
    and safely lived with friends.

Soon David learned the language and
    what plants and fruits to eat,
and any sick who came to him
    he did his best to treat.

He visited the chief again.
    His eyes looked just like new,
yet now his son was sick and he
    did not know what to do.

So David gave him medicine
    and soon he was okay.
The chief then listened keenly to
    what David had to say.

He told the grateful chief about
his God and His great love,
and how the greatest healer of
us all is God above.

Since David's skill at doctoring
    was very much admired,
the many tribes all welcomed him
    to sit around their fires.

They'd tell him stories from their past,
    and then when they were through,
he'd share about his childhood and
    tell Bible stories too.

One night some village men raced past
    with spears and sticks and clubs.
A lion had been killing sheep.
    They searched throughout some shrubs.

As David went off on his own,
    the lion lay in wait.
He did not see it in the woods
    until it was too late.

It jumped on him and grabbed his arm
    in its gigantic jaws.
It lifted David in the air
    and shook him with its claws.

It pressed them down on David's head.
    His agony was great.
The lion shook him yet again.
    He felt his shoulder break.

The village men came running as
    his screaming pierced the air.
They had no choice, they drew their spears
    and killed the lion there.

Though David had been wounded and
    was bloody, bruised and sore,
his faithful God had saved his life,
    which he was grateful for.

He gave the chief the Bible in
a language that he knew,
and soon the chief decided to
become a Christian too.

When he was sixty David died.
He'd faced a lot of fears
and covered forty thousand miles
in over thirty years.

He traveled through thick jungles and
   he went where no one dared.
He showed the tribes the love of God
   through medicine and care.

Like David with his science skills,
   we too can be God's hands,
with any special skills we have,
   in any of God's lands.